SOME TALK OF
BEING HUMAN

SOME TALK OF BEING HUMAN

LAURA FARINA

For Anya —

At Maia's 12th birthday.
Thanks for including me!

Mansfield Press

Copyright © Laura Farina 2014
All rights reserved
Printed in Canada

Library and Archives Canada Cataloguing in Publication

Farina, Laura, 1980-, author
    Some talk of being human / Laura Farina.

Poems.

ISBN 978-1-77126-045-9 (pbk.)

    I. Title.

PS8611.A755S64 2014   C811'.6   C2014-905714-8

Editor for the press: Stuart Ross
Cover painting: Jeannie Richardson
Cover design & typesetting: Stuart Ross
Author photo: Frank Nelissen

The publication of *Some Talk of Being Human* has been generously supported by the Canada Council for the Arts and the Ontario Arts Council.

 Canada Council for the Arts   Conseil des Arts du Canada   

Mansfield Press Inc.
25 Mansfield Avenue, Toronto, Ontario, Canada M6J 2A9
Publisher: Denis De Klerck
www.mansfieldpress.net

For Dan

CONTENTS

A Beginning / 9
Peterborough, Late Spring / 11
Goodbye / 12
A Definition for Snow / 13
Those Girls / 14
2029 / 16
Grade 6, Four O'Clock / 18
Minus Something. Wind Chill. / 19
Customer Satisfaction Survey / 20
Slow / 21
Last Year / 22
Fish / 23
Proverbs / 24
Summer / 26
Family Reunion / 28
Something About Fingers / 30
Night Rain / 31
A Visit from Sarah / 32
A Birthday, a Door, Toronto / 33
The Plants Along the Windowsill / 35
Later, Gator / 36
What the Highway Said to Me / 37
When I Moved Here / 38
Some Ifs / 39
Twelve Lines for Spring / 41
Report from the Field / 42
Love Triangle Astronaut Faces Attempted Murder Charge / 44
Tract / 45
Water / 47
I Have Always Been Good at Collage / 49
Banff / 50
Nature Poem / 51
Camping, Etc. / 52

Solstice Poem / 53

In the Forgotten Corners of the National Parks System / 54

Poem / 55

The Science of Beards and Animals / 56

Raccoon! / 58

An Epic / 59

Rain / 60

A Century of Creepy Stories / 62

I Am So Happy About Your Engagement / 63

Portrait of My Mother Talking on the Phone / 64

Seawall After Brunch / 65

Valentine's Day / 66

For Anne, Who Doesn't Know I Live Here / 67

Cento / 68

Kits Beach / 69

Homecoming / 70

The Waiter Brings Our Order of Hummus / 72

Last Summer / 73

Day / 74

Vine St. / 76

Before the Riot / 77

I Went to Florida / 78

Lullaby / 80

Vancouver, Spring / 81

Dispatches / 82

Love Poem / 84

A BEGINNING

You know of far places
but not of maps.

I know what I've read
about lawn mower maintenance.

You know the history of arguments
against the Dewey decimal system.

I know you can't teach
a cold fog arithmetic.

You know how to read
the outstretched palms of outfielders.

I know the scientific name
for chronic absentmindedness.

You know the board of directors
of the theme park.

I know enough to lock the door
to the fabulous prizes.

You know that it's Thursday.

Wing night.

The night the patron saint
of shoeless horses
approaches the locked door,

shuffles both feet
on the crooked welcome mat
and enters without making a sound.

PETERBOROUGH, LATE SPRING

The sky is the three chords
you know on the guitar.
Repetitive, rhythmic light.

Under it,
those well-written streets,
sagging like couches
on student porches.

Tangled sheets
contain our sweat.
This is known as evidence.

A record spins and spins.

The shadows we cast
on Hunter Street
lug instruments
in awkward cases.

This day is like performing
CPR with a cold.

I swear there was a shortcut,
but I can't seem to find it.
If we walk home the long way,
will you promise not to talk?

GOODBYE

I left the all-night shawarma place.
I left the snowbanks and the mitten in them.
I left the smell of subways in the rain.
I left a library book in a washroom at YVR.
I left a gummy bear in the pocket of my jeans.
I left my sister waiting at the yoga studio.
I left chocolate milk on the aging counter.
I left Peterborough, Ontario.
I left the Quaker Oats factory,
a dark thing in the sunset.

A DEFINITION FOR SNOW

When we went carolling
I slipped a compass inside my mitten

and as our voices rose
in puffs above
the white lawns
of our parents' neighbourhood

you broke into the descant —
high notes in the cold air

and secretly
in the palm of my hand
I pointed the way north.

THOSE GIRLS

Those girls in high school
had better hair.

Waited like smallpox for the bus.
Carried immigrants in their enormous purses.

Were they kind?

They organized bake sales
to raise money for quarantined superheroes.

They painted elaborate portraits
of crumbling statues.

They called their grandparents
by their scientific names.

But did they mean it?

Wore rings to show their fidelity
to uncharted solar systems
and T-shirts condemning
unsafe working conditions for seeing eye dogs.

But, still.

There they were.

With their boyfriends on a bench,
their legs wrapped in twilight,
touching.

Or with hands like a beginner ballet class,
planning a talent show
to celebrate international punctuation:
"The comma is all choreographed
but for the quotation mark
we'll need a smoke machine."

I touched my forehead
with two fingers
and waited to be blessed
by silence.

I am a whisper,
I whispered.
I am a semicolon
in a very long hall.

2029

One robot cannot move his face.
One robot is reprogrammed.

A thick Austrian accent
and muscles
like two round apples
inserted beneath the skin.

On the motorcycle
the cage of his body
hinges around the boy.
They ride, a clamshell
between the semis.

Bullets cause a ripple
but then the lake is still.

A robotic hand
waits in a safe
as quietly as dreams
in a head.

But when they close their eyes
the heroes can only dream
of children made of dust
blown into the faces
of children made of dust.

Everything depends on the boy.
He speaks only in phrases
popular in the 1980s.

Eat me.
Chill out, dickwad.
He says them in dry places
where people live in trailers
on top of automatic weapons.

A man must die for an idea
he is only beginning to have.

Then we are in a room
of chains and lava.
Beneath the skins of the four remaining
are two beating hearts.

Everyone is injured.
Everyone is armed.

There is some talk of being human.
That's what's at stake here.

GRADE 6, FOUR O'CLOCK

You are in your parents' basement.
The wood panelling has eyes
and the shag carpeting is a field of curly hair.
A collection of parts assembled
for the purposes of science.

You are eating processed cheese
with Sierra Bellows.
You unwrap one side of the plastic
flip the cheese over
and expertly unpeel the other side
as if pulling back a shower curtain
to reveal this pale orange slab
naked and cold from the fridge.

Saved by the Bell is on
and you secretly dream
of kissing Zack Morris.
His tall blond hair is taller
and blonder and he carries
a cell phone the size of a forearm.

Sierra Bellows says to you,
"The only people
who have cell phones
are drug dealers."
This is exactly the sort of thing
you get to know
when your father works
for Foreign Affairs
and you lived for a year
in Sri Lanka.

MINUS SOMETHING. WIND CHILL.

It grew cold.
We felt our dislikes strongly.
Blush became unnecessary.
Icicles dangled from mustaches.
Fights broke out over fleece-lined socks.

A woman turned to me:
"This nipping wind blew in from my childhood.
It is just looking for attention.
Ignore it and it will go away."

I wanted to, but it was wailing
like an animal abandoned
and I worried what brought it in the first place.

CUSTOMER SATISFACTION SURVEY

From behind shatterproof glass
he can finally say
what he thinks of me.

It is not all positive.

SLOW

A lizard always coiled
around one finger.
A ring.
Some sort of marriage
to the sun
and long-grain rice
and anything that boils
slowly, anything
that takes time
to get moving in the morning
or has to be thought of
before it is done.

The smell of coffee is like that
and phoning certain people and
I think most arts and crafts
but it's been a while since I tried
to make anything.

I went to the market
and felt the melons,
smelled the berries rotting—
this was in August.

The night before there was singing
and someone played harmonica
much better than I expected.
I stretched out on my bed.
Listened, though it was faint
and far away.
Listened and fell asleep like that.
I was a house unlocked.

LAST YEAR

A well that is neither deep nor wide.
Footprints no one recognizes.
Animals you can call by name.
Songs that begin with a sunset.
Wildlife spotted from behind cold glass.
A crease in a photograph.
A parking lot empty when the mall is closed.
The smell of fast food inside a car.
Eggs for sale on the side of the road.
(Some of them broken.)
Sweaters hanging in a closet, a calendar of days.

FISH

The rod
a fern
and when you reeled
the fish in it was
not large like
we remembered—
the toothed fish
our fathers caught—
but it twisted on the line
like a busy signal.

PROVERBS

A rule you break
is worth two in the beak.

Don't count your clichés
as if they were riches.

Beware the man dressed in plaid
who wants to be paid.

It's when you're most alone
that the cake is done.

You can't pay for a pint
with a pocket of lint.

The rise of the chemise
is the pantsuit's demise.

No duckling has hatched
while being watched.

Until his confession is through
hold back your cough.

To get a tightrope walker to move
you must be willing to shove.

A pint of blood
is worth more than a plate of food.

During prime time, a promise
is always a compromise.

To a blind panda,
everyone is Wanda.

SUMMER

Once there was a meadow
which we called a field.
Did not want to put on airs
and it choked with daisies.

She rang the dinner bell
with the curve of a soup spoon.
Let the screen door slam.

So many mosquitos.
Impossible to sit
in lawn chairs at dusk.
We huddled around the radio
as Alomar rounded second.

Once there was a sandbox. Then
some rotten boards, a pile of sand. A memory
of cousin legs when they were babies
and crouched with shovels around a pail.

To wake in a sleeping bag
and roll over.
To wake as the sun
rolled up the sky.

We devoured meatloaf.
We devoured casserole
with potato-chip topping.

Each of us had
five fingers
for hulling strawberries.
Two feet pressed against
the boat's hull
as we coaxed the Evinrude
to hum.

Down the road
a white church to testify in.
So many eyes
closed for the Lord.

But Euchre was what we worshipped.
Turn down a bower, lose for an hour.
Never trump your partner's ace.

Caught a rock bass on a hook.
Threw it back.

The ring of the party line.
Long short. Long long.
An aunt calling from a distance.
Saying—who all's there this weekend?
A litany of names.

FAMILY REUNION

The sandwiches are crustless!
The salads have layers!
Each woman knows by heart
a recipe called Heavenly or Dreamy or Delightful.
Major ingredient: marshmallows.

Uncle Ralph pulls up
in his white Lincoln Continental.
His two tanned legs
wander down from white shorts
to two white socks pulled parallel.
He opens the passenger door to reveal Aunt Barbara
already laughing.

Uncle Harry tells a joke about
a beautiful woman on the streetcar
but we don't get it.
Auntie Marilyn Todd tells us
she changed our mothers' diapers.

A stooped aunt I don't recognize
calls me by the name of my dead grandmother
and for a moment I see
the spaces in the crowd
were also invited.

And then it's darker
and their voices in the dark night
are a memory of the war,
how they saved their liquor ration—
so sure it would end—
held a victory party
on this very spot
sang these very songs
before they settled down
to invent our parents.

SOMETHING ABOUT FINGERS

You can't trust that TV
won't have some kind of severed finger.
Some guy saying
"I found it! I found the finger!"
These things happen all the time on TV.

Not on TV
the cream goes bad in the fridge.
I stay up for the stillness
at four o'clock.

There is no stillness on TV,
only some girl
putting her finger
into the finger
of a dead man.
This is for the purpose
of fingerprinting.

When the stillness comes
the house will get heavy.
The darkness will press around me
like one of those poems
where a coat
symbolizes a poem.

I open the door
to let in some air.
I am aware
of each separate finger.
Each separate finger
still attached.

NIGHT RAIN

There is a rhythm of wakefulness,
a rhythm of sleep.

Glenn beside me
breathes a crowd of people
moving in and out of trains.
The doors to his dreams
open with caution.

I am chasing sleep around the room.
I think it is on my left side
with one hand under the pillow.

The rhythm of wakefulness
is not a bolting upright.
It is the sound of
water hitting water by a curb.

A darkness other
than the one behind my eyes.

A VISIT FROM SARAH

Small wonder
at a small dog
with its rolls of fat.

I put my hand
on the part of it
that breathes.

A BIRTHDAY, A DOOR, TORONTO

for Glenn

Twenty-seven years ago
you arrived blinking
into a moment you did not understand.

You have moved in
and out of rooms.
You have marvelled at the invention of hinges.

If every birthday
could have a bit with a door.
Someone stumbling through a door,
grabbing at its frame,
someone opening a door
to reveal something private
but funny.

I went to the consecration
of church doors.
The wind took
the priest's breath away—
it floated over a bed of new carrots.

You told me
that the Hebrew word for blessing
literally means more life.

Tonight I lie in bed
and think

of all the doors
you have walked through today.

I think of what the doors
will look like tomorrow.

THE PLANTS ALONG THE WINDOWSILL

I am not here long
but what about the plants
along the windowsill?

That are shocked by cold and wind.
Left and discovered.
Green in the morning
and green in the evening.

Could it be that we
grow into the space provided?
That we range delicately
into whatever light
the afternoon brings?

LATER, GATOR

Careful not to drop
anything, like our last
two drinking glasses,
the half-full jar of mayo.

Will you remember
where the front
porch creaked?
Where the paint peeled
in long strips from
the wall outside the bathroom?

I have drunk more beer
and sat for longer.
I have heard footfalls
when walking alone at night.

Spring comes and goes like weather.

The mail comes at noon.
The toaster toasts one side
of bread more than the other.

Did I ever tell you
you have a warm spot
on the back of your neck?
I discovered it when the weather got cold.
Last night when I pressed my head against it,
you said, Baby, it's late, I'm tired.

WHAT THE HIGHWAY SAID TO ME

We drove through Lansing, Michigan
and the snow was dashing
over the dotted line,
passing us without looking back.

No hitchhikers that evening.
They were inside, smoking, telling
hitchhiking stories.

You turned to me. You said,
It doesn't seem that slippery.
No, I said. It doesn't.
Although I didn't know for sure.

I thought I might roll down the window
to remind us about cold.
Turned the handle
just once
before a rush of snow

hit you and you asked me
what I did that for.

WHEN I MOVED HERE

My feet astride the traffic,
the third home emerges.

Not the silence of the first home,
the orange one.
Where I held my breath
against the neighbours
and warned away
with the hiss of my skirt.
A tent
impenetrable along the wood floor.

Not the comfort of the second home
where I fell into my day
half-dressed,
knowing where I put everything
the night before.
A cup for tea, this home,
and heat in its many forms.
The arms a man has,
the radiator,
those blond-haired children.

The third home, then.

I jingle my house keys
and it comes out
from around the corner,
tail or whatever it has
thumping like a heartbeat.

SOME IFS

There are people
in this city
who are not like you
but who look like you.

I am walking on the Danforth
and see you leaving an organic grocery store.

I walk out onto a diving board at night
surrounded by drowning stars.

Time wells inside my brain
and then a man's voice.

And yesterday I walked past the place where you work
and for the first time it was not outside my city—
it was in my city.
I pictured you rattling around in there.

And the two men drinking coffee in the parking lot
were not late for anything.
They were drinking slow
expressive sips into the sundown.

Careful then.
Stepping out like this
in both our shoes
can be dangerous.

I have not spoken
for days
but today

everyone wants
to tell me
the story
of the first time
they realized
they were funny.

TWELVE LINES FOR SPRING

It was raining hard.
The threat of lightning hid chastised behind a cloud.

A man and his limping dog investigated.
Something lost in the weather.

Both turned to me and said, "Why can't you be
more like your uncle? Welcoming? Inviting confidences?"

"A collector," I agreed. "Like a customs official
telling stories when his shift is done."

The rain, for all our talk, hunched shoulders and continued.
What was lost remained lost.

The words were the wrong ones at the wrong time.
We crumpled and discarded into the receptacle provided.

REPORT FROM THE FIELD

Anagrams lean
in the doorway
like afternoon.

Squint and they
rearrange themselves
into the lunch menu.

The end of the street
beckons.
It is a bookstore
open until seven.

Please tell me there is time.

We walk out together
and the world knows.

We stay home
and perch on furniture.
It becomes harder
to sit through a meal.

Winter finally came
and it was not
heavy or light.
Darkness at five.
Boots in the entrance.

I sighed
because the wind did.

Began reading
books that happened
when prose moved more slowly.

Summer is when I want
everyone to talk.

LOVE TRIANGLE ASTRONAUT FACES ATTEMPTED MURDER CHARGE

It is one thing to love from space.
Cold against the forehead of nothing
is my hand pressed against the glass.

Miles between us are more than a country song.
I left the earth on Friday is what I wrote
in that letter I couldn't send.

Back on earth love is a trench coat
and a wig. Everything less like science.

When I step out of my car
I feel what is heavy in my pocket.

The earth tags along behind me—round and helium.

Everything small
in the face of it.

TRACT

For your baseball team,
I offer
the following suggestions.

Find a man who can see
the back of his own head
and with his peripheral vision
rally mutants and dress them in yellow.

Insist that all batters hum,
while at the plate, ballads,
or tunes to rally the heart
to lost causes. Nothing religious.

For a mascot, I propose
the noble elephant—his
trunk-like bat in one hand,
his bat-like trunk where his nose should be.

On the subject of bats,
might we leave them
in a more tree-like state,
their roots still showing,
small clods of dirt spraying
with each swing?

The fans could be taller, I think.
The beer more Czech.

And the scores that must be settled,
recorded in digits so high that all of us watching
might feel that much is at stake.

Our humanity and hair styles,
our children's too.

That we might leave the stadium, blinking,
still set in the ways we came in with,
but knowing for certain
these are the right ways.

35 to 32 should do it, I think.
Or, 57 to 53, to be safe.

WATER

The difference between me
and water is that I do not evaporate,
boil or flow.

And when I swim
everyone can see clearly
where the lake ends
and I begin.
My legs so white and kicking.

When I argue on the telephone—
I never argue on the telephone.
When the lake calls I don't pick up
and then I see it outside my window
gone flat in the afternoon sun.

The difference between me
and water is that no tall man
ever longed for me on a hot day.
No tall man ever took
one long sip of me
and felt the perfection
of simple things.

And furthermore no family
ever wandered my perimeter
or sat on blankets at the edge of me
eating tuna sandwiches
while I dripped languidly
from the swimsuits
spread on the hood of their car.

The truth is
no one ever said picturesque
or peaceful
or refreshing
or essential
or deep.

I soak my aching feet
inside my silent apartment.

I turn off the tap
when at last my teeth are clean.

I HAVE ALWAYS BEEN GOOD AT COLLAGE

A more compassionate approach
to 1970s fashion is represented
by a sectional sofa.

A holistic way to wait in line
is a white bookcase standing
on a white shag rug.

The finger food at this New Year's party
reminds me of 99-cent hot dogs.

Everyone's hands make
earnest resolutions to the air
they wade through. Everyone's
hands vow to do more yoga.

The new year wanders in
to the sound of sloppy kissing.

It's an end table
knocked against another end table
in the back of a truck.

A brisk flicker
at the edge of the moon,
a sequined dress
dripping to the floor.

I sidle up to a bottle
of filtered water:
"We are not as clean
as we pretend to be."

BANFF

In the mountains
I grow a pair of antlers.
Hang from them
my bright red coat
still dripping with rain.

NATURE POEM

A butterfly
in the rain
will not get
there.

*

The low silhouette of fungus
can often be mistaken
for an exit sign.

*

My grandfather warned me
about nature
where everything
is food.

CAMPING, ETC.

North of here,
a river saunters
between some trees.

Our necks are
white as snowbanks exposed.
Two canoes drifting through days.

You and I have never been camping.

The colours I knew
were greens and browns.
Nobody asked me to stay here.

Leaves are messages
left by loon calls
the day missed.

Light is tinfoil crumpled
in my pocket.

I wonder at the progress of the river at night
when its sound fills the spaces
that arguing left.

SOLSTICE POEM

Three bonfires
and the shadows around them
are people when they go home.

A bottle breaks,
and from somewhere a guitar.

But underneath
a silence
pressing in like mountains
all around.

It is already dark
on the longest day of the year.

IN THE FORGOTTEN CORNERS
OF THE NATIONAL PARKS SYSTEM

Sleek,
it moves
between trees and,
sudden,
it knows
the names
for all the birds.

Even mountains
get a Member of Parliament.

Even nature
wants a voice.

POEM

Alone again,
sighs the mountain.

Alone again,
sighs the bus.

THE SCIENCE OF BEARDS AND ANIMALS

In barbering
there are many words
for facial hair.

Playoff beard
and day-off beard
are two I've heard.

Also cold-chin beard
and works-for-Google beard.

A single drop of water
rests between
thick hairs

as if pausing
on the petal
of something delicate.

In this way,
beards have much in common
with the natural world.

How many raindrops on that fox?

An equation might
calculate thickness.
Rainfall
on a Thursday.
The rate of evaporation.
The deceleration of gentleness.
The number of nervous breaths per minute.

The half-life of any lingering doubts.
The velocity of fingers
raking through fur
on a skittish back.

The gravity involved.

RACCOON!

The highway stretches
away from the raccoon's gaze
and on the left coast—Vancouver!

AN EPIC

I am thinking about KISS.
No—I am thinking about kissing.
A windowless room,
as impenetrable as girls are.

A man walks up to me
on two feet.
When he stops, his feet
stop with him.

He does not carry
sword, axe or amplifier.

He carries in his pocket
one night whispered over
the whisper of a subway.

Then a summons comes
and then some other stuff.
I eat more cereal than I should.

It is dark before he returns
but he bellows victory.

There are dead rock stars
tracked all over the kitchen floor.
Some talk
of breaking old habits.

When I finally bed him
we both speak
like fantasy novels.

RAIN

Rain is the memory of a well,
that first long sip

is many leaving a stadium.

Rain is the way
a loon sounds
at night

the way a phone call
breaks up the day
with an endless stream
of consenting hmmms

is dipping the finger
into reheated soup
to touch one cold carrot
just below the surface.

Rain is the forearm
of the graceful substitute teacher

is the background story
you know is a lie

is the countdown
to the end
of your dental insurance.

Rain is writing
the letter *w* over
until it becomes foreign

is running the index finger
forever over maps

is the space
on a bookshelf
left by a book you lent
and won't get back.

Rain is a carelessness
with photographs

is counting the number
of Emilys you know
oh the excess of Emilys.

Rain is an empty
kindergarten classroom
and its tiny plastic chairs.

A CENTURY OF CREEPY STORIES

Begins with a strange pair
of shoes in the hall.

Contains—
Fist-sized holes in the flower garden.
Eyes neither focused nor sleepy.
An unmistakable draft.

Then, this phrase—
Disappeared in the dead of winter.

There are shuffling sounds
in an empty room,
a typewriter left
on the side of the road.

There are unsaid names.

Questions—
Who tracked dead grass into the empty church?
Why does broken glass always look hungry?

Ends this way—
Three dolls' heads floating
in a swimming pool.

I AM SO HAPPY ABOUT YOUR ENGAGEMENT

She sure is a go-getter—
what with her wit
and third arm
and the way she overcame adversity—
like that time with the lion
and all those schoolchildren
she taught to read.
Her lilting Irish accent
makes lullabies
of shopping lists and I love
how she displays her sense
of humour by wearing T-shirts
with witty slogans—
I'd Kill for a Nobel Peace Prize.
Priceless.

Her way with a tuba
is nifty and she shows
real potential for collaboration
and facilitating change
within our lifetimes. She measures
all ingredients accurately—
a precision
rarely found nowadays.
I like her hair
and the way she wears it.
She's well-read.

You know how you can tell
so much about a person
from her eyes?

PORTRAIT OF MY MOTHER TALKING ON THE PHONE

She is a tulip
pressing a daffodil
to her ear.

SEAWALL AFTER BRUNCH

We walk where others have walked before, but these shoes
belong to us. Were purchased by us for their arch support.
It is grassy where we walk.

We walk and there's a path we follow and a path, too, our
talking follows. The path checks in on everyone we ever knew.
What are they up to now? Are their children still chubby?
Are their vacations still tropical? Are they still doing that thing
with their hair?

There are stones where we walk. Small ones, the grey of
machinery passed over for reinvention. You ask about the
weather. Had I forgotten to mention it?

We talk about what happens when love is over. The space
left by missing books, you say. The square root of some large
number, I say. The standard weight of too much, we agree.
The mountains behind us are too rigid even to be touched
by fog.

We walk past a sculpture pointing at a small spot on the
perfect sun. You say something about winding up a clock
to let it wind back down. I say something about browser
histories. We are, sometimes, in different decades.

Remember the way tears traced the outlines of provinces down
our smooth younger faces? We've known each other so long.

We walk and the sky is blue. So beautiful it holds us—still and
breathing. All that distance. Hello, Saturday, you say. Hello.

VALENTINE'S DAY

Moving in and out
of the house
like a draft

or a worn pair of shoes
untied on the mat
and gone the next morning.

She drinks coffee,
watches gloved workers
unload flowers
from a white truck,

petals dislodged
by the rain.

FOR ANNE, WHO DOESN'T KNOW I LIVE HERE

Ever since I found out
you live in town
I have seen you
everywhere.

Forming your hand
into the shape
of an orange,

reaching
into a stack
of oranges
in the grocery store,

pulling out an orange.

You live in this city, too,
I say to orange-loving you.

CENTO

How exciting it is,
a big rock flies close to the earth
bursting with its pressure and
the desperate scent of Febreeze.

It must be telepathy.
The saleslady
is round. And wet. And warm inside.

What is the sign for unloveliness?
My formula for determining Doris Lessing?
Climbing on the furniture?
The flowers that I left in the ground?

Sometimes I think I know nothing about sex.

KITS BEACH

The sun dips
like soft serve
into chocolate.

The man with the red backpack
places sushi
in the centre of his mouth.

Bikes strewn,
carcasses
we're saving for later.

Ha ha,
says the girl in yellow sneakers.
Ha ha.

HOMECOMING

1.

Rising up behind us
as red loaves of bread—
the coast of your childhood.

The tide walking in
is purposeful and punctual
and soon the shore is behind us
and we are standing in water
over our ankles.

As you describe a sandcastle
washed flat ten years ago—
its moat
and battlements; its flag
and flagpole

we roll up our pant legs,
wade back
to the temporary shore.

2.

The Acadian Heritage Site's
interactive visitor centre
is full of maps and headphones.

We press buttons
to hear actors
read from historical documents.

These days I am always thinking
about home furnishings.
Arranging over and over
upholstered objects in space.

We have lunch
with your high school friends.
They are on the organizing committee
of the harvest festival parade.

Say—are you liking it out there in Vancouver?

I move french fries
around on my plate.

Remember how cassette tapes
used to start with an electronic hum?

THE WAITER BRINGS OUR ORDER OF HUMMUS

There was good news today
about the future of bangs.

It is not as bad as we'd imagined.

My knee touches
your knee
under the table.

Our eyes meet
over grilled pita wedges.
Crumbs dandruff
from my mouth;
my fingers trace beige lines
on the table that dreams
of being rustic.

When I think of the number of times
I've wished I could draw.

When I think of the number
of sketches of you
I could have sold at craft fairs,
looking out a submarine window
or caught in a moment with a fox.

Do you remember that time we went up a mountain?
Or just after,
that time we came down a mountain?
All those miraculous days, my darling.
All those incredible journeys.

LAST SUMMER

That was the summer
squirrels fucked
in our attic,
the sound of bones
knocking bones
in a squirrelskin bag.

We thumped our empty palms on the ceiling.

We thought back to nights spent in cheap motels.

That summer the moon
was a shark
swimming in dark water.
Your face on our balcony
a pale thing floating.

DAY

9 am:
Junk mail recycled.
Slippers stepped out of
and doors locked behind.

11:30 am:
Invitations to the invasion sent out.
Clank of mailbox closing,
an echo from another time.

Noon:
How sunlight touches sidewalk
is a private matter
between sunlight and the sidewalk.

2 pm:
Brown things
step aside
for green things.

4:45 pm:
Winds have already parted
all the hair
they can part for one day.

5:30 pm:
Interview
with a lonely
piece of highway.

9 pm:
This window
might open.
This sky
might spill
and pool.

VINE ST.

The ocean
laps
at the feet
this street
dangles.

BEFORE THE RIOT

This city feels like
it's being crammed
into a very small suitcase.

This city feels like
a dark sort
of carry-on luggage,

like less than
100 mL of someone's tears.

Everywhere
silence invades
on skates
but we no longer care
for skates.

I watch as a man pads
across the street in sock feet,
picks up his panting
golden retriever
—yellow in the empty intersection—
and carries it
safely back inside.

I WENT TO FLORIDA

It was hot.
Much of the food was deep-fried.

I got sunburned
while taking an architectural walking tour
of South Beach.

My toes in the sand
felt like stunted American worms
yearning to be free.

A man in a toll booth told me to have a blessed holiday.
A coconut fell from a coconut tree.

The sun turned the sky the colour of a mixed drink.
I watched a Montessori teacher smoke pot.

The thought occurred to me—
we are all dangling above the open mouth
of the ocean.
It was terrifying for a moment.

A cat jumped through a flaming hoop.
Shadows began to look like mouse ears.

When the radio came on,
someone had replaced the songs
with the sound of fish breathing.

I drank sea water until I felt ill.
I lost sunglasses in three historic buildings.
I ate key lime pie in moving vehicles.

In the darkness,
I thought I saw an alligator wink.

When the wind came up,
the sand beat a hasty departure.

Floridians are an inventive people
when it comes to sorbet.
It's amazing what they can do with animatronics.

The highway was a line between two oceans
and what was washed up on those beaches
was mine to keep.

All the diners were shiny
and inside them, people called me ma'am.
I became programmed to salivate
at the sound of ketchup bottles
hitting Formica tables.

A cruise ship pulling out of port
seemed too large to float,
an island severed from its umbilical cord.

I never once thought about soup.

LULLABY

The houses all around
are tucked in bed
and dreaming of other houses.

The ones you see in magazines.
The ones that watch celebrities sleep.

Traffic is a sigh the city heaves
and bridges sag with exhaustion.
Their stomachs touch the ocean.

Hush, now.
Yesterday is tiptoeing across your lawn,
spray-painting concrete walls with silence,
casting outdated shadows.

Hush, now.
I will stay right here
and play solitaire on my computer
until tomorrow comes.

VANCOUVER, SPRING

A cherry tree
and further down the block
another
and down the block
another

DISPATCHES

1.

A bathtub holds
water,
a foot,
a thought.
Deer by the river
and outside
snow.

2.

Floral patterns
cling to the furniture
of Catholics
I have known
and liked.

3.

Dave says,
I am 80% water.
Really. 80% water.
His smile floats.
The river enunciates.

4.

That thing about
how the truth is beautiful.

I broke the tiger.

5.

In a doorless house
a kettle boiling
fogs the window.

A yearbook of faces
in this morning's clouds.

6.

Where I come from
it is always this cold
and our mittened hands
are forever
on our soft ears.

7.

The stems of Queen Anne's lace.
The rough things our fingers remember.

8.

The code breaker
died on a Thursday.

9.

By the time you get this message
the bath will already be cold.

LOVE POEM

Perched on a stool,
as one bespectacled gargoyle over Paris,
my love.

As fine in a red shirt as on a cold night
those two arms can sink the ships of my heart,
send up fireworks to celebrate the drowning of stars.

This part, my heart,
played with toes, not fingers
by a ukulele orchestra,
each instrument
crafted by a master
and sold at auction.

I outbid, I did.

On afternoons
when the lake is stretched out under July heat
my heart is under the surface
disturbing the fish.

Tell it plain—
you cannot go around making a girl ineffectual like this,
cataloguing for a lover's almanac:
quantities of light,
the subtle angle of collar bones,
all things whispered.

Prediction: another season of missed appointments.

All this by way of saying
still crazy about you.
Still!

ACKNOWLEDGEMENTS

I would like to thank the editors of the following publications, where some of these poems first appeared: *This Magazine*, *Syd & Shirley*, *ottawater*, *The Week Shall Inherit the Verse*, *Hava LeHaba* and *Strange Material: Storytelling Through Textiles*.

Many of these poems were written in the presence of Leanne Prain, Susannah Smith, Kat Siddle, Tara Williston and Erin Ashenhurst. I'm thankful for their company, generosity and willingness to push when necessary.

"Some Ifs" and "Water" were written from prompts offered by Julie Hartley. "Those Girls" was written after seeing a photograph by Frank Nelissen. "Tract" was inspired by a poem of the same name by William Carlos Williams, as filtered through the genius brain of Glenn Clifton. "Banff," "Nature Poem," "Solstice Poem" and "In the Forgotten Corners of the National Park System" were written in studios in the Leighton Artists' Colony at the Banff Centre. "I Am So Happy About Your Engagement" was written during a writing workshop lead by Elizabeth Bachinsky.

"Something About Fingers" was performed as part of Waxwing Theatre's production of Flight. Thanks to Eleonore Prokop, Celeste Dickson, Daniel Poulin, Jeanette Hedley, Jordi Hepburn, Laura Jeanne Wicksted and Neil Silcox.

"Grade 6, Four O'Clock," "Twelve Lines for Spring" and "Cento" were all written during one of Stuart Ross's mind-bending Poetry Boot Camps. "Camping Etc.," also written during a Boot Camp, was composed while listening to a poem by John Ashbery.

"Seawall After Brunch" is for Jeca Glor-Bell.

Thanks to everyone who offered their feedback, encouragement and time, most especially: Chris Gully, Evan Hazenberg, Glenn Clifton, Beth Follett, Helen Guri, Stewart Cole, David Reibetanz, Jessica Drucker, Christianne Hayward, Dylan Taylor and the writers at the Lyceum and Centauri Summer Arts Camp.

Thanks to Denis De Klerck of Mansfield Press for his incredible support.

Thanks from the bottom of my heart to Stuart Ross. Since the first time I read one of his poems he has consistently challenged my ideas about poetry, and my writing is better for it. I am grateful for his thoughtful edits and overwhelming cheerleading abilities.

Thanks to my family: Janet, Chummer and Heather Farina, the Taylors, the Withams, the Thompsons and the Duffins.

Thanks most of all to my husband, Dan Bates, who claims to know nothing about poetry, but who always listens anyway.

Laura Farina's first book of poetry, *This Woman Alphabetical* (Pedlar Press, 2005), won the Archibald Lampman Award, given to the best poetry book published in Ottawa. She grew up in Ottawa, and then gradually made her way west. She now lives in Vancouver.

Other Books From Mansfield Press

Poetry

Leanne Averbach, *Fever*
Nelson Ball, *In This Thin Rain*
Nelson Ball, *Some Mornings*
Gary Barwin, *Moon Baboon Canoe*
George Bowering, *Teeth: Poems 2006–2011*
Stephen Brockwell, *Complete Surprising Fragments of Improbable Books*
Stephen Brockwell & Stuart Ross, eds., *Rogue Stimulus: The Stephen Harper Holiday Anthology for a Prorogued Parliament*
Diana Fitzgerald Bryden, *Learning Russian*
Alice Burdick, *Flutter*
Alice Burdick, *Holler*
Jason Camlot, *What The World Said*
Margaret Christakos, *wipe.under.a.love*
Pino Coluccio, *First Comes Love*
Marie-Ève Comtois, *My Planet of Kites*
Dani Couture, *YAW*
Gary Michael Dault, *The Milk of Birds*
Frank Davey, *Poems Suitable for Current Material Conditions*
Pier Giorgio Di Cicco, *The Dark Time of Angels*
Pier Giorgio Di Cicco, *Dead Men of the Fifties*
Pier Giorgio Di Cicco, *The Honeymoon Wilderness*
Pier Giorgio Di Cicco, *Living in Paradise*
Pier Giorgio Di Cicco, *Early Works*
Pier Giorgio Di Cicco, *The Visible World*
Salvatore Difalco, *What Happens at Canals*
Christopher Doda, *Aesthetics Lesson*
Christopher Doda, *Among Ruins*
Glenn Downie, *Monkey Soap*
Rishma Dunlop, *The Body of My Garden*
Rishma Dunlop, *Lover Through Departure: New and Selected Poems*
Rishma Dunlop, *Metropolis*
Rishma Dunlop & Priscila Uppal, eds., *Red Silk: An Anthology of South Asian Women Poets*
Ollivier Dyens, *The Profane Earth*
Jaime Forsythe, *Sympathy Loophole*
Carole Glasser Langille, *Late in a Slow Time*
Suzanne Hancock, *Another Name for Bridge*
Jason Heroux, *Emergency Hallelujah*
Jason Heroux, *Memoirs of an Alias*
Jason Heroux, *Natural Capital*
John B. Lee, *In the Terrible Weather of Guns*
Jeanette Lynes, *The Aging Cheerleader's Alphabet*
David W. McFadden, *Be Calm, Honey*
David W. McFadden, *Shouting Your Name Down the Well: Tankas and Haiku*

David W. McFadden, *What's the Score?*
Leigh Nash, *Goodbye, Ukulele*
Lillian Necakov, *The Bone Broker*
Lillian Necakov, *Hooligans*
Peter Norman, *At the Gates of the Theme Park*
Peter Norman, *Water Damage*
Natasha Nuhanovic, *Stray Dog Embassy*
Catherine Owen & Joe Rosenblatt, with Karen Moe, *Dog*
Corrado Paina, *The Alphabet of the Traveler*
Corrado Paina, *The Dowry of Education*
Corrado Paina, *Hoarse Legend*
Corrado Paina, *Souls in Plain Clothes*
Stuart Ross et al., *Our Days in Vaudeville*
Matt Santateresa, *A Beggar's Loom*
Matt Santateresa, *Icarus Redux*
Ann Shin, *The Last Thing Standing*
Jim Smith, *Back Off, Assassin! New and Selected Poems*
Jim Smith, *Happy Birthday, Nicanor Parra*
Robert Earl Stewart, *Campfire Radio Rhapsody*
Robert Earl Stewart, *Something Burned on the Southern Border*
Carey Toane, *The Crystal Palace*
Priscila Uppal, *Summer Sport: Poems*
Priscila Uppal, *Winter Sport: Poems*
Steve Venright, *Floors of Enduring Beauty*
Brian Wickers, *Stations of the Lost*

Fiction

Marianne Apostolides, *The Lucky Child*
Sarah Dearing, *The Art of Sufficient Conclusions*
Denis De Klerck, ed., *Particle & Wave: A Mansfield Omnibus of Electro-Magnetic Fiction*
Paula Eisenstein, *Flip Turn*
Sara Heinonen, *Dear Leaves, I Miss You All*
Christine Miscione, *Carafola*
Marko Sijan, *Mongrel*
Tom Walmsley, *Dog Eat Rat*

Non-Fiction

George Bowering, *How I Wrote Certain of My Books*
Rosanna Caira & Tony Aspler, *Buon Appetito Toronto*
Denis De Klerck & Corrado Paina, eds., *College Street–Little Italy: Toronto's Renaissance Strip*
Pier Giorgio Di Cicco, *Municipal Mind: Manifestos for the Creative City*
Amy Lavender Harris, *Imagining Toronto*
David W. McFadden, *Mother Died Last Summer*

For a complete list of Mansfield Press titles, please visit mansfieldpress.net